MY CLASS

ENJOYS

COOKING

Ruth Thomson

meets

Philip Jones

Photography: Maggie Murray

Franklin Watts
London/New York/Toronto/Sydney

Christopher Rawlins CE
Primary School

MY CLASS
ENJOYS
COOKING

It's cooking today.
I love cooking.
We hurry to put on our aprons
and wash our hands.

We fetch everything we need
and put it on the table.
I wonder what we're going to make today?

We ask Carly's mum.
She comes every week
to help us cook.
'We will make coconut
cakes,' she says,
as she ties back
Carly's hair.

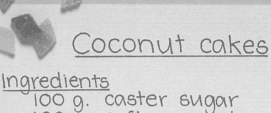

Coconut cakes

Ingredients
100 g. caster sugar
100 g. soft margarine
2 eggs
100g. self raising flour
20g. coconut

Utensils
Scales • Mixing bowl • Wooden spoon • Metal spoon • Cup • Fork • Teaspoon • Bun tin • 12 paper cases

1. Weigh out butter and sugar. Put in bowl and mix with wooden spoon until creamy.

2. Break eggs into cup. Whisk with fork. Add to butter and sugar mixture. Stir until well mixed in.

3. Weigh flour. Sieve into the mixture.

4. Weigh coconut. Tip into the mixture.

5. Fold in flour and coconut with metal spoon.

6. Put cake cases into bun tin. Spoon mixture into cake cases. Bake at 350°F (160°C or gas mark 4) for 25 minutes. Remove carefully from oven using oven gloves. Leave to cool.

Barry and Jenny
weigh the sugar
and the margarine.

Lucie mixes them
together
in a big bowl.

I carefully crack
two eggs into
a jug.

I beat them
until they go frothy.

Jenny pours the eggs into the bowl
a little at a time.
Lucie mixes them in well.

I weigh out the flour
and sieve it
into the mixture.
Barrie spoons in
some coconut.

We take it in turns
to fold them in
with a spoon.

I put the pretty
paper cases
in the bun tins.

Jenny drops
a spoonful
of mixture
into each one.

Now it's time to tidy up.
Licking our fingers is the best bit.

Carly's mum puts the cakes
into the hot oven.
She says they will take
twenty minutes to bake.

While we're waiting, we wash up.
The water is very soapy.
I wipe everything dry
and stack it in a pile.

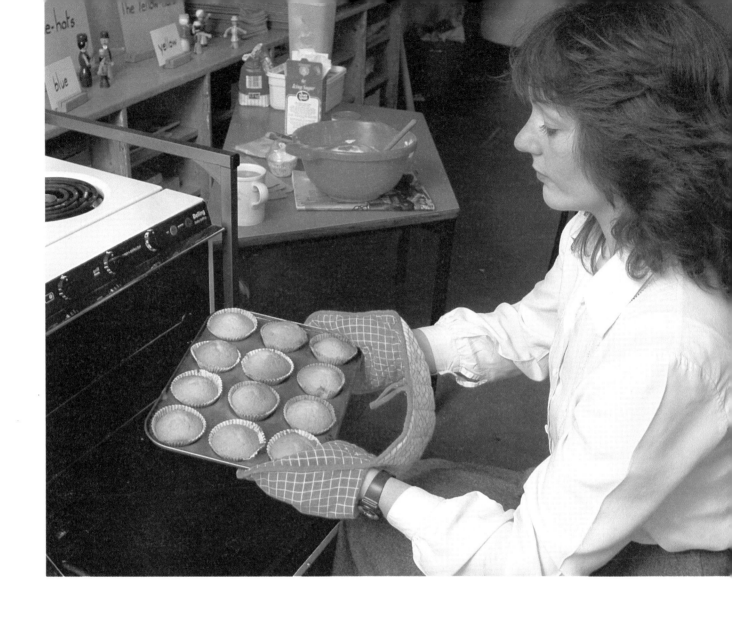

The cakes are ready.
Carly's mum puts on oven gloves
to take the hot tin out of the oven.
They smell delicious.

Now the cakes have cooled,
we can spread on the icing.
I like pink icing the best.

Look how pretty the cakes are now.
Carly's mum says they look too good to eat.
I can't wait to try one.

Fruit Salad

Ingredients	Utensils
2 apples	Board
2 satsumas	Knife
2 bananas	Bowl
2 pears	Spoon
1 grapefruit	Peeler
2 oranges	
Bunch of grapes	

1. Peel bananas, slice and put into bowl.

2. Peel satsumas, separate into segments and put into bowl.

3. Peel grapefruit, separate into segments. Cut each segment in half. Put into bowl.

4. Wash apples and pears. Cut into quarters. Core and slice. Put in bowl.

5. Wash grapes. Cut in half. Take out all the pips. Put grapes into bowl.

6. Cut oranges in half. Squeeze the juice out. Pour juice over salad. Mix well with a spoon.

7. Spoon the fruit salad into little bowls.

Some of the class
go shopping
to buy fresh fruit
for a fruit salad.
They check their
list and pay.

Anar carefully
counts the change.

Back at school, they start making
the fruit salad.
The satsumas are easy to peel.
Bananas are stiffer to open.
Grapefruits are the toughest of all.

Anar separates the satsumas into pieces.

Jeff cuts the bananas into slices.

Damien chops the grapefruit into chunks.

Apples, pears and grapes
don't need peeling.

The children wash
them under the tap
and dry them.

Lucy cuts the grapes
in half.
Ross and Julie chop
their fruits
into little pieces.

Carly stirs the fruit
round in the bowl.
Now it's ready to eat.

Chapatis

Ingredients
1 cup wholemeal flour
1 dessertspoonful vegetable oil
$\frac{1}{4}$ to $\frac{1}{2}$ cup lukewarm water
50g. melted butter

Utensils
Mixing bowl • Rolling pin • Board •
Frying pan • Metal fish slice • metal bowl

1. Mix oil with flour in the bowl.

2. Slowly add water to the flour, mixing with your fingers to make a soft dough.

3. Rub oil on your fingers. Mix the dough into a smooth ball.

4. Divide the dough into ping-pong size balls. Flatten them between your palms.

5. Dust the flattened dough with flour, and roll it into rounds about ¼ cm thick.

6. Melt butter in a metal bowl.

7. Cook in a hot pan for 1 minute. Turn over with fish slice and cook for a further ½ minute. Remove from pan. Pour on melted butter and eat while warm.

Mrs Patel shows us how to make chapatis.
She mixes some oil with some flour
and adds water, a little at a time.
We help her mix them into a soft dough.

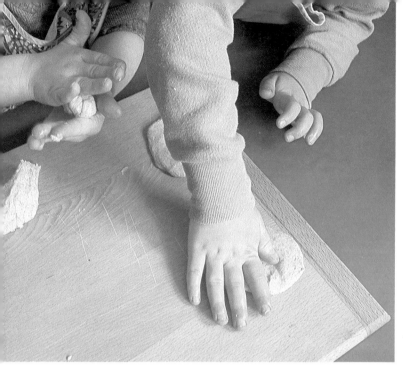

She gives each of us
a small piece.
We roll the dough
between our hands
and flatten it
on the board.

Mrs Patel shows us
how to roll it out.

We watch Mrs Patel
cook the chapatis.
Some of them puff up.

We put a spoonful
of melted butter
on them.

Look at all the food we have made.

We have a tea party on the carpet,
just before going-home time.
I can't wait to tell mum
what we've been doing today.

©1987 Franklin Watts
12a Golden Square
London W1R 4BA

ISBN 0 86313 560 9

Design: Edward Kinsey

The Handi-Read logo appears only on those books
and audio-visual items approved by the National
Library for the Handicapped Child, sponsored by
The Enid Blyton Trust For Children.

The Handi-Read logo may not be reproduced,
stored in a retrieval system or transmitted by any
means, electronic, mechanical, photocopying,
recording or otherwise, without the prior
permission of The Enid Blyton Trust For Children.

The Publishers, author and
photographer would like to thank the
staff and pupils of Gilbert Scott Infant
School, South Croydon. Special thanks
are due to Pauline Everett, head
teacher; Dorothy Graham, class
teacher; Mary Innes, special needs
teacher; and Siân Evans and Bhadra
Patel, parent helpers. Special thanks are
due to Vic Bowyer, fruiterer and
greengrocer, Addington.

Ruth Thomson has written and
researched a wide range of children's
books. She lives in North London and has
two children.

Printed in Italy